THE FALL OF BABYLON

MORRIS CERULLO

This book or parts thereof may not be reproduced
in any form without the written permission
of Morris Cerullo World Evangelism.

Unless otherwise noted, all Scripture references are from the
King James version of the Bible.

Scripture references marked TAB are from The Amplified Bible
version Copyright © 1965 by Zondervan Publishing House.

Scripture references marked NIV are from the New
International version of the Bible, Copyright © 1973,1978,1984,
by the International Bible Society.

Scripture references marked NAS are from the
New American Standard version of the Bible. Copyright ©
1960,1962,1963, 1968, 1971,1972,1975, 1977
by the Lockman Foundation.

Scripture references marked TLB are from the Living Bible.
Copyright © 1971 by Tyndale House Publishers,
Wheaton, Illinois 60187. All rights reserved.

Published by Morris Cerullo World Evangelism
Copyright © 2000 San Diego, California
Printed in the United States of America

Morris Cerullo World Evangelism
P.O. Box 85277 San Diego, CA 92186-5277

Morris Cerullo World Evangelism of Canada
P.O. Box 3600 Concord, Ontario L4K1B6

Morris Cerullo World Evangelism
P.O. Box 277, Hemel Hempstead, HERTS HP2 7DH

Tel: (858) 277-2200
Website: www.mcwe.com

Cover artwork is used by permission.
It is from a series of illustrations by
Pat Marvenko Smith ©1982, 1992 on the Book of Revelation,
available as art prints and visual teaching aids.
A free brochure is available from
Revelation Productions 1-800-327-7330
Website: www.revelationillustrated.com

TABLE OF CONTENTS

INTRODUCTION V

CHAPTER ONE:
    THE IDENTITY OF BABYLON 1

CHAPTER TWO:
    THE SCARLET-COLORED BEAST 5

CHAPTER THREE:
    WARRING AGAINST THE LAMB 9

CHAPTER FOUR:
    THE FALL OF BABYLON 13

CHAPTER FIVE:
    THE FATE OF THE APOSTATE CHURCH 19

CHAPTER SIX:
    CHARACTERISTICS OF AN APOSTATE CHURCH 23

INTRODUCTION

THE FALL OF BABYLON
The Coming Collapse Of The World System
Revelation chapters 17-18

This is the ninth in a series of twelve books in which we are opening the prophecies of the endtimes revealed to the Apostle John and recorded in the Book of Revelation.

In chapters 1 through 11, the Apostle John received successive revelations of the final days of time. He viewed tremendous scenes of worship in Heaven, the opening of the book with seven seals, and the sounding of the seven trumpets as God's judgment was poured out on the world.

In Revelation chapters 12-14, John introduced seven important personages:

The Sun-clothed Woman, representing Israel.

The Dragon, representing Satan.

The Man-child, representing Jesus Christ.

Michael, representing the angels.

The Beast out of the Sea, who is the world dictator.

The Beast out of the Earth, a religious leader who is a false prophet and supports the world dictator.

144,000 Representing the Remnant, saved out of the Tribulation.

As Revelation chapter 14 opened, we saw the 144,000 on Mt. Zion with the Heavenly Father's name written in their foreheads, who have overcome by the blood of the Lamb and the word of their testimony, God's spiritual Israel.

Suddenly – right in the midst of this glorious scene, three angels fly through the air with three final warnings to those who remain on the earth...

...THE FIRST ANGEL proclaims the Gospel to the world giving mankind a final opportunity to repent and worship the true and living God (Revelation 14:6-7).

...THE SECOND ANGEL announces the coming fall of Babylon the Great, the apostate church (Revelation 14:8). Those who have compromised with the world, those who have polluted the Church, and those who have perverted the Word of God are warned of the destruction that is soon to come upon them.

...THE THIRD ANGEL warns of coming destruction upon all those who take the mark of the Antichrist: Revelation 14:9-11.

Then John witnessed horror and devastation as the seven vials of God's wrath were poured out in chapters 14-16...

...THE FIRST VIAL: Malignant sores (Revelation 16:2).

...THE SECOND VIAL: The sea turns to blood (Revelation 16:3).

...THE THIRD VIAL: Rivers and drinking water sources turn to blood (Revelation 16:4-7).

...THE FOURTH VIAL: The sun scorches with intense heat (Revelation 16:8-9).

...THE FIFTH VIAL: Darkness (Revelation 16:10-11).

...THE SIXTH VIAL: The River Euphrates dries up and demonic forces are loosed in the earth (Revelation 16:12).

...THE SEVENTH VIAL: A great earthquake occurs; Jerusalem is divided; and the fall of Babylon nears (Revelation 16:17-21).

In this booklet we will be examining the fall of Babylon which was foretold by the second angel announcing woes to come:

And there followed another angel, saying, Babylon is fallen, is fallen, that great city, because she made all nations drink of the wine of the wrath of her fornication. (Revelation 14:8)

As the seventh vial of God's wrath is poured out, *"...great Babylon came in remembrance before God, to give unto her the cup of the wine of the fierceness of his wrath"* (Revelation 16:19).

CHAPTER 1

THE IDENTITY OF BABYLON

As chapter 17 opens, one of the seven angels who had been given the responsibility of pouring out the vials of God's wrath upon the wicked, called out to John:

> ...Come up hither; I will shew unto thee the judgment of the great whore that sitteth upon many waters: With whom the kings of the earth have committed fornication, and the inhabitants of the earth have been made drunk with the wine of her fornication. (Revelation 17:1-2)

Suddenly, John is carried away in the spirit into the wilderness where he sees a very unusual sight:

> So he carried me away in the spirit into the wilderness: and I saw a woman sit upon a scarlet coloured beast, full of names of blasphemy, having seven heads and ten horns. And the woman was arrayed in purple and scarlet colour, and decked with gold and precious stones and pearls, having a golden cup in her hand full of abominations and filthiness of her fornication: And upon her forehead was a name written, MYSTERY, BABYLON THE GREAT, THE MOTHER OF HARLOTS AND ABOMINATIONS OF THE EARTH. And I saw the woman drunken with the blood of the saints, and with the blood of the martyrs of Jesus: and when I saw her, I wondered with great admiration. (Revelation 17:3-6)

Archaeologists tell us that ancient Babylon was the cradle of modern civilization. Located on the shores of the Euphrates River,

Chapter 1

the ruins of this city have revealed some of the oldest documents of past generations. This city was founded by Nimrod, who was a rebel before the Lord. The city generated some of the greatest wickedness ever known to mankind and in ancient days Satan seemed to make Babylon the capital of his evil operations.

From these headquarters started false religion, man's attempt for self-government in defiance of the will of God, and city dwellings for commercial and social purposes contrary to the commandment of God to "be fruitful, multiply, and replenish the earth." These evils substituted counterfeit solutions to problems that would ordinarily lead men to God.

The first few verses of Chapter 17 reveal to us an awful scene portraying through symbols two great forces, one religious and the other governmental.

This vision comes from one of the seven angels who had the seven bowls and – although it is not stated by John – the context locates this judgment scene as taking place in the middle of the Tribulation.

Ten details are provided about this woman. She is…

1. "The great harlot."

2. "That sitteth upon many waters."

3. "With whom the kings of the earth have committed fornication."

4. "And the inhabitants of the earth have been made drunk with the wine of her fornication."

5. "A woman (in the wilderness) sitting upon a scarlet colored beast."

6. "Arrayed in purple and scarlet."

7. "Bedecked with gold and precious stones."

8. "Having a golden cup in her hand, full of abominations and filthiness of her fornication."

9. "Upon her forehead was a name written, MYSTERY, BABYLON THE GREAT, MOTHER OF HARLOTS AND ABOMINATIONS OF THE EARTH."

10. "Drunk with the blood of the saints and with the blood of the martyrs of Jesus."

Sitting upon a scarlet-colored beast, this drunken harlot is clothed in purple and scarlet and wearing all types of jewelry made of gold, pearls, and precious stones. In her hand she holds a golden cup. On her head she wears a band with the title; *"Mystery, Babylon the great, the mother of harlots and abominations of the earth."*

Who is this mother of harlots? What is the identity of Babylon the great? What is the meaning of the beast upon which she sits?

Even before we receive the angel's interpretation of this vision, it is clear that we are not dealing with a human being, for no one woman could commit fornication with the kings of the earth, nor could a woman be drunk with the blood of the saints and martyrs.

One of the main rules for Bible interpretation is that when the literal meaning of a Scripture makes common sense, we seek no other meaning. In this case a literal woman does not make common sense, therefore we seek another meaning.

To discover the meaning of this passage, we must first look back into the Old Testament record where references to a harlot were always used to signify religious apostasy. The prophet Isaiah referred to Israel as "the faithful city" that had become a harlot:

> *How is the faithful city become an harlot! It was full of judgment; righteousness lodged in it; but now murderers. (Isaiah 1:21)*

Jeremiah identified the backslidden people of God who had been corrupted by heathen nations as a harlot. He said, *"Have you seen what backsliding Israel has done? She...played the harlot"* (Jeremiah 3:6, TAB).

This same message was repeated by Isaiah, Jeremiah, Ezekiel, Hosea, Joel, Amos, and Micah as Israel continued to pollute themselves through idolatry and intermarrying with heathen nations.

The harlot is referred to in Revelation 17:18 as *"that great city that reigneth over the earth"* and in verse five she is wearing a band on her head which identifies her as Babylon the great.

This "harlot" does not represent a physical city, but rather a spiritual condition. Ancient Babylon had a worldwide reputation

CHAPTER 1

for its luxury, vice, and corruption. It was considered the center of false religions and pagan gods. This reference to the city of Babylon is made to emphasize the corruption of the apostate church. The woman seated on the scarlet-colored beast is the apostate church which has committed spiritual adultery with the world.

Thus we see that there are two rival women at the endtime. Both claim to love Christ. One is the true Church – the bride of Christ (Revelation 19:7-9). The other is the apostate false church, the great harlot of Babylon.

The kings of the earth have committed fornication with this woman. This tells us that the false church of the endtime will have a great influence on the nations of the world. The church loves the world and the world loves her. But the Bible warns:

> *Love not the world, neither the things that are in the world. If any man love the world, the love of the Father is not in him. (1 John 2:15)*

"The inhabitants of the earth...made drunk" refers to the false doctrines and teachings of the apostate church.

Stop and think for a moment: Are you in a church that is a growing part of the apostate world church? Have you been made "drunk" by her wine so that you don't even recognize what is happening to you?

Note that the great harlot has a royal external appearance, but her cup – that which she offers to others – is filled with abominations. That the cup is golden shows that her teachings may outwardly seem to be beautiful, moral, and godly, but from that glistening cup comes only filth.

The "mystery" of the woman is made clear to us by the name on her forehead. "Babylon the Great" reveals that the final apostate world church system will have its roots in the false religions of history.

The name "Babylon," however, refers to two systems in the end times. It refers to the final apostate religious system which we are discussing and it also refers to the political and commercial networks during the Tribulation that will be entwined with the one-world system...

...And that brings us to the mystery of the scarlet colored beast...

4   THE IDENTITY OF BABYLON

THE SCARLET-COLORED BEAST

The scarlet-colored beast in Revelation 17 is the same beast described in Revelation 13:1 which we have identified as the Antichrist:

> And the angel said unto me, Wherefore didst thou marvel? I will tell thee the mystery of the woman, and of the beast that carrieth her, which hath the seven heads and ten horns. The beast that thou sawest was, and is not; and shall ascend out of the bottomless pit, and go into perdition: and they that dwell on the earth shall wonder, whose names were not written in the book of life from the foundation of the world, when they behold the beast that was, and is not, and yet is. And here is the mind which hath wisdom. The seven heads are seven mountains, on which the woman sitteth. And there are seven kings: five are fallen, and one is, and the other is not yet come; and when he cometh, he must continue a short space. And the beast that was, and is not, even he is the eighth, and is of the seven, and goeth into perdition. And the ten horns which thou sawest are ten kings, which have received no kingdom as yet; but receive power as kings one hour with the beast. These have one mind, and shall give their power and strength unto the beast. (Revelation 17:7-13)

Five important details are given regarding the beast upon which the harlot is seated. THE BEAST…

1. Is "full of names of blasphemy" (v. 3)

2. "Having seven heads" (v. 3)

3. "And ten horns" (v. 3)

4. It "...carrieth her" (v. 7)

5. It "...was, and is not, and shall ascend out of the bottomless pit, and go into perdition" (v. 8)

The facts that this beast existed in the past, cannot now be seen, but shall appear again coming out of the bottomless pit-ñ-all point to Satan. Satan existed in the past, cannot be visibly seen now, but will be released on this world in the future in the physical forms of the Antichrist and false prophet whose political and economic systems will at first support the "woman" [the apostate church].

The seven heads on this beast upon which the harlot was sitting symbolize seven mountains. This undoubtedly refers to the city of Rome which was built on seven hills and was considered the capital of the Roman Empire. In John's day, it was the center of persecution against Christians.

The ten horns on these seven heads are the ten nations comprising the revived Roman Empire which will join together with the Antichrist during the great tribulation. These ten horns are those ten kings portrayed in Daniel 2:42 and forty-four as the ten toes of the statue that we studied about in the last book in this series. Daniel 7:24-28 portrays these as ten horns which are ten kings and speaks of the Antichrist coming as another horn:

> *And the ten horns out of this kingdom are ten kings that shall arise: and another shall rise after them; and he shall be diverse from the first, and he shall subdue three kings. And he shall speak great words against the most High, and shall wear out the saints of the most High, and think to change times and laws: and they shall be given into his hand until a time and times and the dividing of time. But the judgment shall sit, and they shall take away his dominion, to consume and to destroy it unto the end. And the kingdom and dominion, and the greatness of the kingdom under the whole heaven, shall be given to the people of the saints of the most High, whose kingdom is an everlasting kingdom, and all dominions shall serve and obey him. Hitherto is the end of the matter...(Daniel 7:24-28)*

This passage corresponds with the verses in Revelation 17:12-13 which show that these ten kings follow the Antichrist in his final hour of power. "These have one mind" indicate that these ten end-time kings give complete allegiance to the Antichrist.

In Revelation 17:6, John saw the harlot "drunken with the blood of the saints, and with the blood of the martyrs of Jesus." Because of her alliance with the Antichrist during his persecution of the saints, the apostate church will be guilty of the blood of those who are martyred for their faith in Jesus Christ. In Revelation 18:24, we read that: "...*in her was found the blood of prophets, and of saints, and of all that were slain upon the earth."*

CHAPTER 3

WARRING AGAINST THE LAMB

The ten nations, which have aligned themselves with the Antichrist, will eventually join together and make war with the Lamb:

> *These shall make war with the Lamb, and the Lamb shall overcome them: for he is Lord of lords, and King of kings: and they that are with him are called, and chosen, and faithful. (Revelation 17:14)*

The ten kings and the Antichrist will make war against the Lamb, Jesus Christ. They will persecute those who turn to Christ, and the persecution will be especially fierce during the final three years of the Tribulation.

Yet Christ – the Lamb of God – shall overcome them! This is accomplished in several ways...

1. The persecution of the Antichrist and his kings is overcome by Christ's Blood sacrifice at Calvary atoning for the sins of those who turn to Him as their Savior:

> *And they overcame him by the blood of the Lamb, and by the word of their testimony; and they loved not their lives unto the death. (Revelation 12:11)*

2. Christ is victorious because death is swallowed up in victory:

> *...And I saw...the souls of them that were beheaded for the witness of Jesus, and for the word of God, and which had not worshipped the beast, neither his image, neither had received his mark upon their foreheads, or in their hands; and they lived and reigned with Christ a thousand years. (Revelation 20:4)*

CHAPTER 3

3. Jesus delivers pre-tribulation believers from the hour of temptation:

> *Because thou hast kept the word of my patience, I also will keep thee from the hour of temptation, which shall come upon all the world, to try them that dwell upon the earth. (Revelation 3:10)*

4. Jesus saves a remnant from death by preserving them during the Tribulation:

> *And the woman fled into the wilderness, where she hath a place prepared of God, that they should feed her there a thousand two hundred and threescore days. (Revelation 12:6)*

> *And to the woman were given two wings of a great eagle, that she might fly into the wilderness, into her place, where she is nourished for a time, and times, and half a time, from the face of the serpent. (Revelation 12:14)*

5. At the end of the seven-year period, Jesus comes to battle at Armageddon and destroys the Antichrist, his followers, and his armies – we'll learn more about this in the next book in this series.

6. At the final judgment, Jesus does not permit the followers of the Antichrist to enter the Millennial Kingdom;

> *When the Son of man shall come in his glory, and all the holy angels with him, then shall he sit upon the throne of his glory: And before him shall be gathered all nations: and he shall separate them one from another, as a shepherd divideth his sheep from the goats: And he shall set the sheep on his right hand, but the goats on the left. Then shall the King say unto them on his right hand, Come, ye blessed of my Father, inherit the kingdom prepared for you from the foundation of the world...Then shall he say also unto them on the left hand, Depart from me, ye cursed, into everlasting fire, prepared for the devil and his*

> angels...And these shall go away into everlasting punishment: but the righteous into life eternal. (Matthew 25:31-34, 41,46)

THE CALLED OUT ONES

The ones who return with Jesus to do battle are the "called out ones, the chosen, the faithful." They are the ones who have remained faithful to God, despite the apostate church and despite persecution during the Tribulation.

When Jesus Christ returns in great power and majesty with these called and chosen saints, He will conquer the Antichrist, the false prophet, and all those who are aligned with them in a great and final victory!

The angel then reveals to John the meaning of the waters:

> And he saith unto me, The waters which thou sawest, where the whore sitteth, are peoples, and multitudes, and nations, and tongues. (Revelation 17:15)

All peoples, multitudes, nations, and tongues are affected by this apostasy. In the end, however, the ten nations – represented by the ten horns – will turn on the apostate church and destroy her:

> And the ten horns which thou sawest upon the beast, these shall hate the whore, and shall make her desolate and naked, and shall eat her flesh, and burn her with fire. For God hath put in their hearts to fulfil his will, and to agree, and give their kingdom unto the beast, until the words of God shall be fulfilled. And the woman which thou sawest is that great city, which reigneth over the kings of the earth. (Revelation 17:16-18)

Once again, we see who is really in control. GOD IS THE ONE IN CONTROL! The Antichrist, the ten-nation confederacy, the one-world government – none of them are in control. It is God Who causes the ten kingdoms to agree to give their authority to the Antichrist and who causes them to eventually attack and destroy the apostate church.

THE FALL OF BABYLON

In chapter 18, John continues his description of the destruction of the apostate church. He sees an angel with great power, authority, and glory coming down from heaven, declaring with a mighty voice...

> ...*Babylon the great is fallen, is fallen, and is become the habitation of devils, and the hold of every foul spirit, and a cage of every unclean and hateful bird. For all nations have drunk of the wine of the wrath of her fornication, and the kings of the earth have committed fornication with her, and the merchants of the earth are waxed rich through the abundance of her delicacies. (Revelation 18:2-3)*

The angel comes to show John the ruination of the Babylonian system's latter day metropolis, the commercial emporium of the world.

The pronouncement speaks of a future event as already having taken place. This was the method used in Isaiah 53 when the prophet described the first advent of the Messiah as if already accomplished. Thus he wrote seven-hundred years before Christ...

> *But he was wounded for our transgressions, he was bruised for our iniquities: the chastisement of our peace was upon him; and with his stripes we are healed. (Isaiah 53:5)*

Here we find the same basic language dealing with the fall of latter – day Babylon as Isaiah used seven-hundred years B.C. to speak of the fall of the ancient Babylonian kingdom:

> *Behold, I will stir up the Medes against them, which shall not regard silver; and as for gold, they shall not*

> *delight in it. Their bows also shall dash the young men to pieces; and they shall have no pity on the fruit of the womb; their eye shall not spare children. And Babylon, the glory of kingdoms, the beauty of the Chaldees" excellency, shall be as when God overthrew Sodom and Gomorrah. It shall never be inhabited, neither shall it be dwelt in from generation to generation: neither shall the Arabian pitch tent there; neither shall the shepherds make their fold there. But wild beasts of the desert shall lie there; and their houses shall be full of doleful creatures; and owls shall dwell there, and satyrs shall dance there. And the wild beasts of the islands shall cry in their desolate houses, and dragons in their pleasant palaces: and her time is near to come, and her days shall not be prolonged. (Isaiah 13:17-22)*

The ancient Babylonian empire was vanquished by an invasion of the Medes and Persians in 536 B.C. (Isaiah 13:17; Daniel 5:28-31), while the Babylon destroyed in Revelation 18 is destroyed in a sudden devastation by fire at the time of the pouring out of the Seventh Bowl of Wrath.

Following this declaration, John hears another loud voice from heaven warning the people of God:

> *And I heard another voice from heaven, saying, Come out of her, my people, that ye be not partakers of her sins, and that ye receive not of her plagues. For her sins have reached unto heaven, and God hath remembered her iniquities. (Revelation 18:4-5)*

This admonition was a warning, not only to believers in the Early Church who were living when John wrote the Book of Revelation, but it is also a warning to all true believers today. We cannot be joined together with the apostate church and partake of her sins, compromise with the world, and expect to escape the judgment of God.

Some of those who have turned to God have, as is evident from the command here, remained in this evil city. The heavenly voice commands them to "COME OUT!" The incentive for obedience is "that ye be not partakers of her plagues."

The Bible warns us:

> Be ye not unequally yoked together with unbelievers: for what fellowship hath righteousness with unrighteousness? and what communion hath light with darkness? And what concord hath Christ with Belial? or what part hath he that believeth with an infidel? And what agreement hath the temple of God with idols? for ye are the temple of the living God; as God hath said, I will dwell in them, and walk in them; and I will be their God, and they shall be my people. Wherefore come out from among them, and be ye separate, saith the Lord, and touch not the unclean thing; and I will receive you, And will be a Father unto you, and ye shall be my sons and daughters, saith the Lord Almighty. Having therefore these promises, dearly beloved, let us cleanse ourselves from all filthiness of the flesh and spirit, perfecting holiness in the fear of God. (2 Corinthians 6:14-7:1)

Today, God is appealing for His people to come out, just as the angel appealed to Lot (Genesis 19:12-25). This is the cry of the Spirit that is going forth even today to the Church...

...Come out from the world.

...Separate yourself from sin.

...Get ready – Jesus is coming!

This Babylonish – Antichrist system has reveled in sin, and it seemed as if God had overlooked it. With its sudden destruction, however, it will be apparent that God has "remembered her iniquities."

> ...and great Babylon came in remembrance before God, to give unto her the cup of the wine of the fierceness of his wrath. (Revelation 16:19)

Chapter 4

Because of the sins committed by the apostate church, God's judgments will come upon her quickly and harshly. The ten nation alliance will be used by God to destroy the apostate church. In "one day, death, and mourning, and famine," will come upon her:

> Reward her even as she rewarded you, and double unto her double according to her works: in the cup which she hath filled fill to her double. How much she hath glorified herself, and lived deliciously, so much torment and sorrow give her: for she saith in her heart, I sit a queen, and am no widow, and shall see no sorrow. Therefore shall her plagues come in one day, death, and mourning, and famine; and she shall be utterly burned with fire: for strong is the Lord God who judgeth her. (Revelation 18:6-8)

At the start of this chapter, the harlot and the beast rode together but eventually the Antichrist and his ten kings turn in hatred upon the harlot. From this passage, we see that the united apostate world church will support the evil Antichrist in his rise to power, during the first three years of the Tribulation but that somewhere along the line, the Antichrist, his kings, and their supporting economic and political system will turn against this apostate church.

Perhaps this will occur in connection with the Abomination of Desolation and the persecution that follows? Perhaps the Antichrist will turn on the harlot church because she rivals him for power? In any case, we see a progressively worsening relationship and a thoroughly complete destruction. But remember – all of this is in accord with God's plan of the ages! It was foretold by John in this awesome revelation centuries ago.

The false church is somewhat synonymous with the ancient ruling city of the earth. She is called, BABYLON so in God's sight this system becomes basically the same as Babel – Babylon, a system of total rebellion against God.

The world mourns at the destruction of the harlot – the apostate church! The kings, merchants, and men of influence who have yielded to her temptations and have committed adultery with her all mourn...

CHAPTER 4

And the kings of the earth, who have committed fornication and lived deliciously with her, shall bewail her, and lament for her, when they shall see the smoke of her burning...And cried when they saw the smoke of her burning, saying, What city is like unto this great city! And they cast dust on their heads, and cried, weeping and wailing, saying, Alas, alas, that great city, wherein were made rich all that had ships in the sea by reason of her costliness! For in one hour is she made desolate. (Revelation 18:9,18-19)

THE FATE OF THE APOSTATE CHURCH

You will remember that in the Lord's message to the church in Thyatira He reproved them for allowing the false prophetess, Jezebel, to remain in their church because she was seducing believers into fornication and sacrificing to idols:

> *Notwithstanding I have a few things against thee, because thou sufferest that woman Jezebel, which calleth herself a prophetess, to teach and to seduce my servants to commit fornication, and to eat things sacrificed unto idols. And I gave her space to repent of her fornication; and she repented not. Behold, I will cast her into a bed, and them that commit adultery with her into great tribulation, except they repent of their deeds. And I will kill her children with death; and all the churches shall know that I am he which searcheth the reins and hearts: and I will give unto every one of you according to your works. (Revelation 2:20-23)*

This is an example of the fate of an apostate church!

Revelation chapter 18 also describes the fate of the end-time apostate church, Babylon the harlot:

> *And the merchants of the earth shall weep and mourn over her; for no man buyeth their merchandise any more: The merchandise of gold, and silver, and precious stones, and of pearls, and fine linen, and purple, and silk, and scarlet, and all thyine wood, and all manner vessels of ivory, and all manner vessels of most precious wood, and of brass, and iron, and marble, And cinnamon, and odours, and ointments, and frankincense,*

CHAPTER 5

and wine, and oil, and fine flour, and wheat, and beasts, and sheep, and horses, and chariots, and slaves, and souls of men. And the fruits that thy soul lusted after are departed from thee, and all things which were dainty and goodly are departed from thee, and thou shalt find them no more at all. The merchants of these things, which were made rich by her, shall stand afar off for the fear of her torment, weeping and wailing, And saying, Alas, alas, that great city, that was clothed in fine linen, and purple, and scarlet, and decked with gold, and precious stones, and pearls! For in one hour so great riches is come to nought. And every shipmaster, and all the company in ships, and sailors, and as many as trade by sea, stood afar off, And cried when they saw the smoke of her burning, saying, What city is like unto this great city! And they cast dust on their heads, and cried, weeping and wailing, saying, Alas, alas, that great city, wherein were made rich all that had ships in the sea by reason of her costliness! For in one hour is she made desolate. Rejoice over her, thou heaven, and ye holy apostles and prophets; for God hath avenged you on her. And a mighty angel took up a stone like a great millstone, and cast it into the sea, saying, Thus with violence shall that great city Babylon be thrown down, and shall be found no more at all. And the voice of harpers, and musicians, and of pipers, and trumpeters, shall be heard no more at all in thee; and no craftsman, of whatsoever craft he be, shall be found any more in thee; and the sound of a millstone shall be heard no more at all in thee; And the light of a candle shall shine no more at all in thee; and the voice of the bridegroom and of the bride shall be heard no more at all in thee: for thy merchants were the great men of the earth; for by thy sorceries were all nations deceived. (Revelation 18:11-23)

A study of this passages reveals the terrible fate that awaits those who join themselves together with the world's system and commit spiritual adultery. Each of these judgments may be

CHAPTER 5

applied spiritually to the Church today, in addition to their specific application to the harlot, Babylon:

…A double return of the evil they commit:

> *Reward her even as she rewarded you, and double unto her double according to her works: in the cup which she hath filled fill to her double. (Revelation 18:6)*

…Economic devastation:

> *And the merchants of the earth shall weep and mourn over her; for no man buyeth their merchandise any more. (Revelation 18:11)*

…Loss of that which was lusted after:

> *And cinnamon, and odours, and ointments, and frankincense, and wine, and oil, and fine flour, and wheat, and beasts, and sheep, and horses, and chariots, and slaves, and souls of men. (Revelation 18:13)*

…Loss of joy:

> *And the voice of harpers, and musicians, and of pipers, and trumpeters, shall be heard no more at all in thee; and no craftsman, of whatsoever craft he be, shall be found any more in thee; and the sound of a millstone shall be heard no more at all in thee. (Revelation 18:22)*

…Spiritual darkness:

> *And the light of a candle shall shine no more at all in thee; and the voice of the bridegroom and of the bride shall be heard no more at all in thee: for thy merchants were the great men of the earth; for by thy sorceries were all nations deceived. (Revelation 18:23)*

…Sudden destruction:

> *Therefore shall her plagues come in one day, death, and mourning, and famine; and she shall be utterly*

> *burned with fire: for strong is the Lord God who judgeth her. (Revelation 18:8)*
>
> *...Alas, alas, that great city Babylon, that mighty city! For in one hour is thy judgment come. (Revelation 18:10)*

...Total destruction:

> *And a mighty angel took up a stone like a great millstone, and cast it into the sea, saying, Thus with violence shall that great city Babylon be thrown down, and shall be found no more at all. (Revelation 18:21)*

John sees a strong angel pick up a stone, similar to a millstone. Millstones were four to five feet in diameter, one foot thick, and weighed thousands of pounds. This mighty angel, with a sweep of his hand, hurled this millstone into the sea and declared, *"Thus with violence shall that great city Babylon be thrown down, and shall be found no more at all"* (verse 21). The destruction of Babylon will be complete, swift, and final.

The treasures of the wicked are gone. Isn't this the irony of iniquity? Sin deludes us into thinking that we can have great treasures, but in the end they all turn to ashes. We must always remember the words of Jesus who warned...

> *Lay not up for yourselves treasures upon earth, where moth and rust doth corrupt, and where thieves break through and steal: But lay up for yourselves treasures in heaven, where neither moth nor rust doth corrupt, and where thieves do not break through nor steal: For where your treasure is, there will your heart be also. The light of the body is the eye: if therefore thine eye be single, thy whole body shall be full of light. But if thine eye be evil, thy whole body shall be full of darkness. If therefore the light that is in thee be darkness, how great is that darkness! No man can serve two masters: for either he will hate the one, and love the other; or else he will hold to the one, and despise the other. Ye cannot serve God and mammon. (Matthew 6:19-24)*

CHARACTERISTICS OF AN APOSTATE CHURCH

As we face the closing days of time, it becomes increasingly important for us to be able to recognize the signs of an apostate church.

In Revelation chapter 18, we are given a detailed description of the apostate church:

> How much she hath glorified herself, and **lived deliciously**, so much torment and sorrow give her: for she saith in her heart, **I sit a queen, and am no widow, and shall see no sorrow**. Therefore shall her plagues come in one day, death, and mourning, and famine; and she shall be utterly burned with fire: for strong is the Lord God who judgeth her. And the kings of the earth, who have **committed fornication** and lived deliciously with her, shall bewail her, and lament for her, when they shall see the smoke of her burning, Standing afar off for the fear of her torment, saying, Alas, alas, that great city Babylon, that mighty city! For in one hour is thy judgment come…And the **fruits that thy soul lusted after** are departed from thee, and all things which were dainty and goodly are departed from thee, and thou shalt find them no more at all. The merchants of these things, which were **made rich by her**, shall stand afar off for the fear of her torment, weeping and wailing, And saying, Alas, alas, that great city, that was clothed in fine linen, and purple, and scarlet, and decked with gold, and precious stones, and pearls! For in one hour so **great riches** is come to nought. And every shipmaster, and all the company in ships, and sailors, and as many as trade by sea, stood afar off, And cried when they saw the smoke of her

*burning, saying, What city is like unto this **great city**! And they cast dust on their heads, and cried, weeping and wailing, saying, Alas, alas, that **great city**, wherein were **made rich** all that had ships in the sea by reason of her costliness! For in one hour is she made desolate. Rejoice over her, thou heaven, and ye holy apostles and prophets; for God hath avenged you on her. And a mighty angel took up a stone like a great millstone, and cast it into the sea, saying, Thus with violence shall that great city Babylon be thrown down, and shall be found no more at all. And the voice of harpers, and musicians, and of pipers, and trumpeters, shall be heard no more at all in thee; and no craftsman, of whatsoever craft he be, shall be found any more in thee; and the sound of a millstone shall be heard no more at all in thee; And the light of a candle shall shine no more at all in thee; and the voice of the bridegroom and of the bride shall be heard no more at all in thee: for thy merchants were the great men of the earth; for **by thy sorceries were all nations deceived. And in her was found the blood of prophets, and of saints, and of all that were slain upon the earth.** (Revelation 18:7-24)*

The bold-faced portions in this passage, combined with other New Testament references, reveal the following characteristics which mark an apostate church:

1. **The apostate church will reject sound doctrine. The Apostle Paul warned:**

   For the time is coming when (people) will not tolerate (endure) sound and wholesome instruction, but having ears itching (for something pleasing and gratifying), they will gather to themselves one teacher after another to a considerable number, chosen to satisfy their own liking and to foster the errors they hold, And will turn aside from hearing the truth and wander off into myths and man-made fictions. (2 Timothy 4:3-4, TAB)

The apostate church will pollute the Word and introduce heresies, refusing to acknowledge Christ as the Son of God. Peter said:

> ...there will be false teachers among yourselves, who will subtly and stealthily introduce heretical doctrines destructive – heresies – even denying and disowning the Master Who bought them, bringing upon themselves swift destruction. (2 Peter 2:1, TAB)

2. **The apostate church will be materially rich, but spiritually poor**: Note the passages in bold face in the previous passage drawn from Revelation 18:7-24... **She was rich, made others rich, and lived deliciously.** God's message to such a church is...

> Because thou sayest, I am rich, and increased with goods, and have need of nothing; and knowest not that thou art wretched, and miserable, and poor, and blind, and naked: I counsel thee to buy of me gold tried in the fire, that thou mayest be rich; and white raiment, that thou mayest be clothed, and that the shame of thy nakedness do not appear; and anoint thine eyes with eyesalve, that thou mayest see. (Revelation 3:17-18)

3. **The apostate church will be full of Christians who follow after their own lustful desires:**

> Know this first of all, that in the last days mockers will come with their mocking, following after their own lusts. (2 Peter 3:3, NAS)

> This know also, that in the last days perilous times shall come. For men shall be lovers of their own selves, lovers of pleasures more than lovers of God. (2 Timothy 3:1-2,4)

4. **The apostate church will have a form of godliness, but will deny the true power of God:**

> *Having a form of godliness, but denying the power thereof: from such turn away. (2 Timothy 3:5)*

5. **The apostate church will be full of Christians who have lost their first love**: They will be more in love with the world and its material possessions than they are the things of God (Revelation 18:15-16):

   > *Love not the world, neither the things that are in the world. If any man love the world, the love of the Father is not in him. (1 John 2:15)*

6. **The apostate church will reject God's prophets**:

   > *And in her was found the blood of prophets, and of saints, and of all that were slain upon the earth. (Revelation 18:7-24)*

7. **The apostate church will deceive the nations**:

   > *...for by thy sorceries were all nations deceived. (Revelation 18:23)*

8. **The apostate church will be filled with evil, sorcery, and fornication**:

   > *With whom the kings of the earth have committed fornication, and the inhabitants of the earth have been made drunk with the wine of her fornication...having a golden cup in her hand full of abominations and filthiness of her fornication. (Revelation 17:2,4)*

   > *For all nations have drunk of the wine of the wrath of her fornication, and the kings of the earth have committed fornication with her...(Revelation 18:3)*

9. **The apostate church will compromise to avoid persecution**: This church is accepted by the world and rejects the idea of suffering and persecution... "*I sit a queen, and am no widow, and shall see no sorrow*" (Revelation 18:7).

A GREAT FALLING AWAY

The Apostle Paul warned that before Christ returns, there will be a great falling away:

> *Now we beseech you, brethren, by the coming of our Lord Jesus Christ, and by our gathering together unto him, That ye be not soon shaken in mind, or be troubled, neither by spirit, nor by word, nor by letter as from us, as that the day of Christ is at hand. Let no man deceive you by any means: for that day shall not come, except there come a falling away first, and that man of sin be revealed, the son of perdition; Who opposeth and exalteth himself above all that is called God, or that is worshipped; so that he as God sitteth in the temple of God, shewing himself that he is God. (2 Thessalonians 2:1-4)*

The Greek word for "falling away" is "apostasia," which means "apostasy; a revolt; rebellion." Throughout history, there have been periods of great apostasy in the Church. Many Christians have been deceived or disillusioned and have fallen away. Others have compromised by adopting the world's standards and sin has crept into the Church. Many have followed after their own lusts and have denied the faith.

In these verses, Paul warns that before Christ returns, there will be a time of apostasy of such great proportions that it will be known as the final apostasy. It will be a time of FINAL REBELLION and rejection of God.

You may wonder, "Brother Cerullo, how can this be? The Church is on the verge of experiencing the greatest outpouring of the Holy Spirit that the world has ever known."

Yes, it is true that we are experiencing a great outpouring of the Holy Spirit; thousands of souls are being won into the Kingdom of God; miracles of healing and deliverance are occurring on a great scale around the world; the Church is experiencing great spiritual breakthroughs; the Church is growing and we are seeing breakthroughs in satellite technology that will enable us to cover every nation of the world with the resurrection power of Jesus Christ.

Chapter 6

Simultaneously, while we are witnessing signs, wonders, and this great outpouring of His Spirit, we are also witnessing sin on an unprecedented scale. In the Church, spiritual lukewarmness and unconcern for the lost is rampant.

There are tens of thousands of people, right now, who are straddling the fence, with one foot in the world and one foot in the Church. There are Christians today who are walking after their own lusts and saying, "*Where is the promise of his coming?*" (2 Peter 3:3-4).

Some of them may say that they believe Jesus is coming, but their actions prove otherwise. They have become so materialistic and selfish that they are more interested in acquiring things than winning souls.

While the move of the Holy Spirit will grow stronger and stronger, this apostasy and rebellion against God will continue to grow until there will be a clear line of separation drawn between the true Body of Christ and professing Christians, between good and evil, and between God's divine system and Satan's counterfeit system.

In 1957, in Lima, Ohio, God gave me a vision where I saw a great end time outpouring of the Holy Spirit. At the same time, I saw the Church and this coming time of separation. God told me: "There will come a time when My Church no longer will be able to walk a line in the middle and hold onto both sides – the Church and the world, the moving of the Holy Spirit and complacency. There will be a distinct line that will be drawn between My people and those who are not willing to pay the price. Those who want the real moving of the Holy Spirit will be clearly distinguished from anybody else."

Many believers and denominations will defect to the one-world church to escape persecution. Those who want to escape the trials will have to compromise or else there will be no escape. During this time, those who want to stand true to Jesus Christ and be part of the real Body of Christ will be tested. They will face the fire of persecution.

I believe, with all my heart, that there will be many martyrs for the cause of Jesus Christ in the not too distant future. We have already seen many in oppressed nations like China, Iran, Iraq, etc. Even in the United States – at a school called Columbine – young people were shot and killed because of their confession of Jesus Christ.

Once that final line is drawn and there is a separation between the real Body of Christ and the harlot apostate church, God will send strong DELUSION upon all those who refuse the truth and rebel against Him:

And for this cause God shall send them strong delusion, that they should believe a lie. (2 Thessalonians 2:11)

The word "delusion" means "the act of misleading the mind; to impose on; to deceive or trick." God will cause the minds of those who have rejected the truth and have delighted in wickedness to be deceived into believing Satan's lies and his counterfeit system. All those who refused to hear and accept the truth will be judged and condemned.

Do you see why it is so important for you, as a soldier in God's end-time army, to warn others of this coming judgment and point them to the Way, the Truth and the Life before it is too late?

Heed the warning – separate yourself from the world! Prepare yourself for Christ's coming. Destruction and judgment are coming upon this counterfeit harlot church. The plagues of God's wrath are going to be poured out upon it.

That is why today, God is issuing the call: "Come ye out from among her and be ye separate. Be cleansed. Be purified. Return unto Me. Do not compromise My Word. I am calling you to walk holy and undefiled before Me. Do not pollute yourself with a love for the world and its pleasures. Do not be carried away and follow after your own lusts. Seek My face – seek truth with your whole heart. Come to Me. I will cleanse you, I will perfect you, I will separate you. Feed upon My Word, for it will provide a strong and sure foundation for your feet. You will not stumble or be afraid but you will go forth from My Presence clothed with My power. My glory will be upon you. All this will I do for My people who will humble themselves. Return unto Me, and walk holy before Me."

These warnings concerning the coming apostasy and God's judgment upon the apostate church are given to you so that you will be ON GUARD – SPIRITUALLY ALERT – against the deception and seducing spirits that are working in the Church today.

Chapter 6

In these closing days of time, ask God to give you a spirit of discernment so you will not be led away from the truth!

Be sure to obtain your copy of the next book in this powerful New Millennium 2000 Prophetic Series, *Armageddon And The New Millennium*.

In book ten of this series you will learn...

...What happens in Heaven when apostate Babylon is destroyed.

...The purposes of the three final end-time battles.

...Details of the millennial reign of Jesus Christ.

...Why Satan will be loosed after the thousand years.

...How to prepare for the marriage supper of the Lamb.

Morris Cerullo World Evangelism
P.O. Box 85277 San Diego, CA 92186-5277

Morris Cerullo World Evangelism of Canada
P.O. Box 3600 Concord, Ontario L4K1B6

Morris Cerullo World Evangelism
P.O. Box 277, Hemel Hempstead, HERTS HP2 7DH

Tel: (858) 277-2200
Website: www.mcwe.com